DO BUSINESS WITH THE MINA!

Understand the One Job Jesus Gave You to Do

Editors
Dara Ekanger
Joni K. Wileman Bock

Illustrator
Arash Jahani

Typesetting
Olivier Darbonville

DO BUSINESS WITH THE
MINA!

Understand the One Job
Jesus Gave You to Do

by

JACOB BOCK

CONTENTS

DO BUSINESS WITH THE
MINA!

*Understand the One Job
Jesus Gave You to Do*

Why should you read this book?

Check the statements below that are true for you.

☐ I'm not sure exactly what the will of God is for my life.

☐ I have accepted Christ and know that Jesus has forgiven me, but something is still lacking. Sometimes I say, "Is this all there is to the Christian life?"

☐ I sometimes feel bored as a Christian.

☐ I rarely or never share the Gospel. I don't consider it my ministry.

☐ I want to hear God say to me on Judgment Day, "Well done, good and faithful servant."

☐ The Parable of the Ten Minas . . . isn't that the same as the Parable of the Talents? What is a mina anyway?

I am glad you are reading this book. If you have checked one or more of these thoughts, I will address these questions and do my best to help you resolve some of these issues.

Why is understanding the Parable of the Ten Minas so important?

So many Christians don't understand their mission as believers. Perhaps they came into Christianity with the idea of just having Jesus as a ticket to Heaven and to avoid Hell. Maybe they have never read or been told they have a mission. Perhaps they understand the mission, but they just aren't active in obeying it. As a result, they live unfulfilled and without much purpose, and they cannot sense God's approval of their lives. In their mind, they hang on to the hope that they will make it to Heaven someday, and maybe God will say to them, "Well done" or maybe "Good enough."

You do not have to live like that! Understanding this parable will solidify your calling as a Christian.

What will you learn in this book?

■ God's will and mission for your life.

■ How you can secure God's approval.

■ What the "Mina" represents.

■ The "one job" Jesus gave you to do.

■ What it means to "do business" with the Mina.

■ What happens to those who don't allow Jesus to rule their lives?

■ Whether you are a faithful servant, an unfaithful servant, or a citizen.

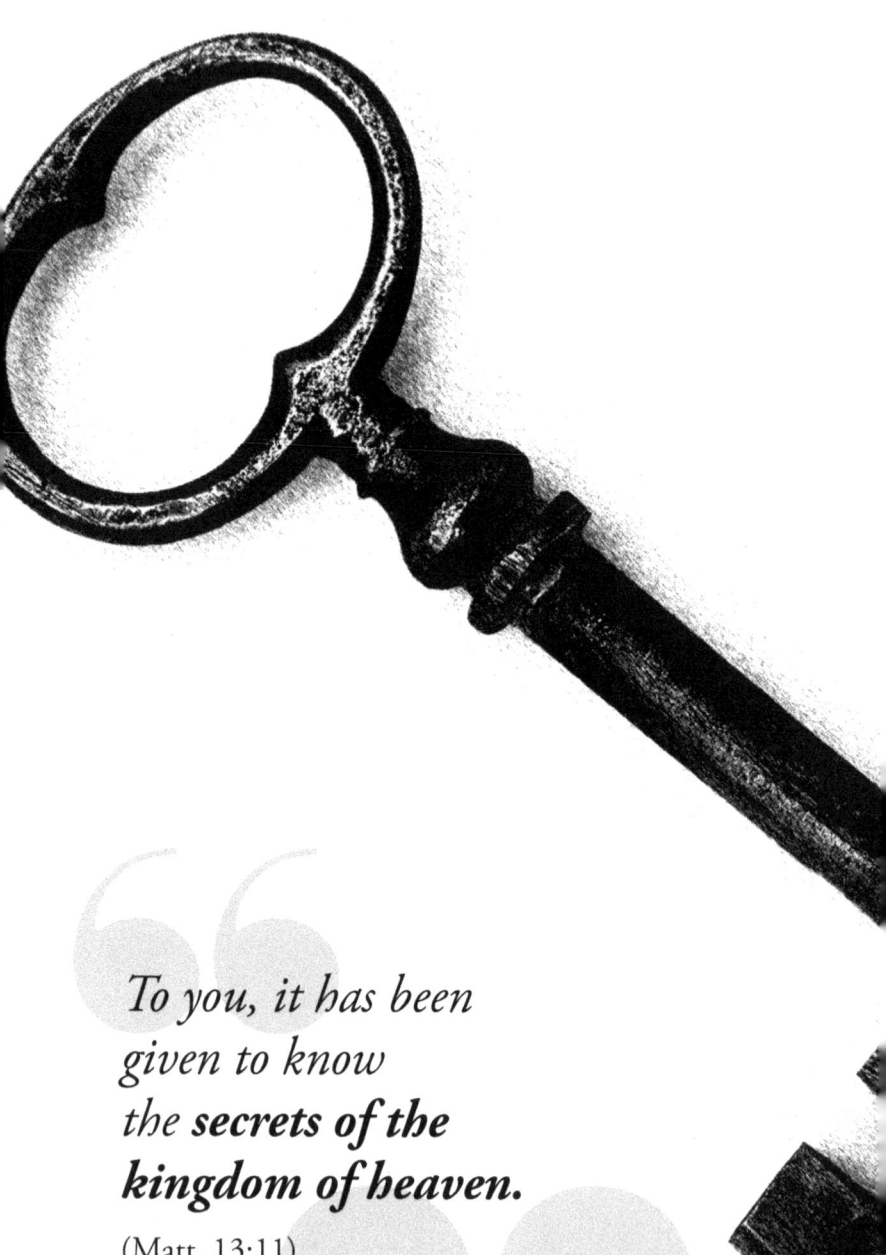

*To you, it has been given to know the **secrets of the kingdom of heaven.***

(Matt. 13:11)

CHAPTER 1

SECRETS OF THE KINGDOM

As Jesus walked this earth, His purpose was to teach principles of the Kingdom of God to the people. One of the ways He did this was to tell parables. These stories about familiar things helped His listeners understand spiritual truths. Most people needed help understanding the meaning of the parables.

Right after Jesus told the Parable of the Sower, for example, His disciples began scratching their heads and saying, "Why do you speak to them in parables?" Even His closest followers were having difficulty understanding this story. Then Jesus said something incredibly profound:

To you, it has been given to know the **secrets of the kingdom of heaven**, but to them, it has not been given. For to the one who has, more will be given, and he will have an abundance, but from the one who has not, even what he has will be taken away.[1]

I am sure it thrilled Jesus to reveal these mysteries to His disciples when they asked for an explanation. And for two thousand years, He has revealed spiritual truth to those willing to ask.

In March 2020, I read the Parable of the Ten Minas in Luke 19 and wondered, "What in the world does that mean?" That is what my human mind asked. Little was I to know that Jesus was about to begin unfolding a Kingdom secret to me!

Over the next year, the Holy Spirit began to reveal to me the secrets of the Kingdom of Heaven in this parable. Insight and understanding began pouring in. I started writing down all the gold nuggets of truth He was revealing in the story. The list grew from one to a hundred and then to over two hundred. *"For to the one who has, more will be given."*

I shook my head and thought, "Amazing! This parable is a gold mine."

I would ask my closest friends, "Have you ever seen

---

1   Matthew 13:11–13

this? Isn't this intense? Can you imagine if I preached this? Wow. I'm not so sure what would happen. It kinda scares me."

A year later, I mustered up the courage to preach the message for the first time at a church in Madrid, Spain. I was nervous. What would happen when I shared the secrets of the Kingdom with those who had ears to hear?

That morning, God poured out his Spirit powerfully, and the altars were filled with repentant followers of Christ. From that day forward, they committed to being faithful servants and dedicated their lives to doing business with the Mina.

The Lord has helped me write this book; now it is your turn to understand this great mystery! May He give you ears to hear, eyes to see, and a heart to obey the secrets He will reveal.

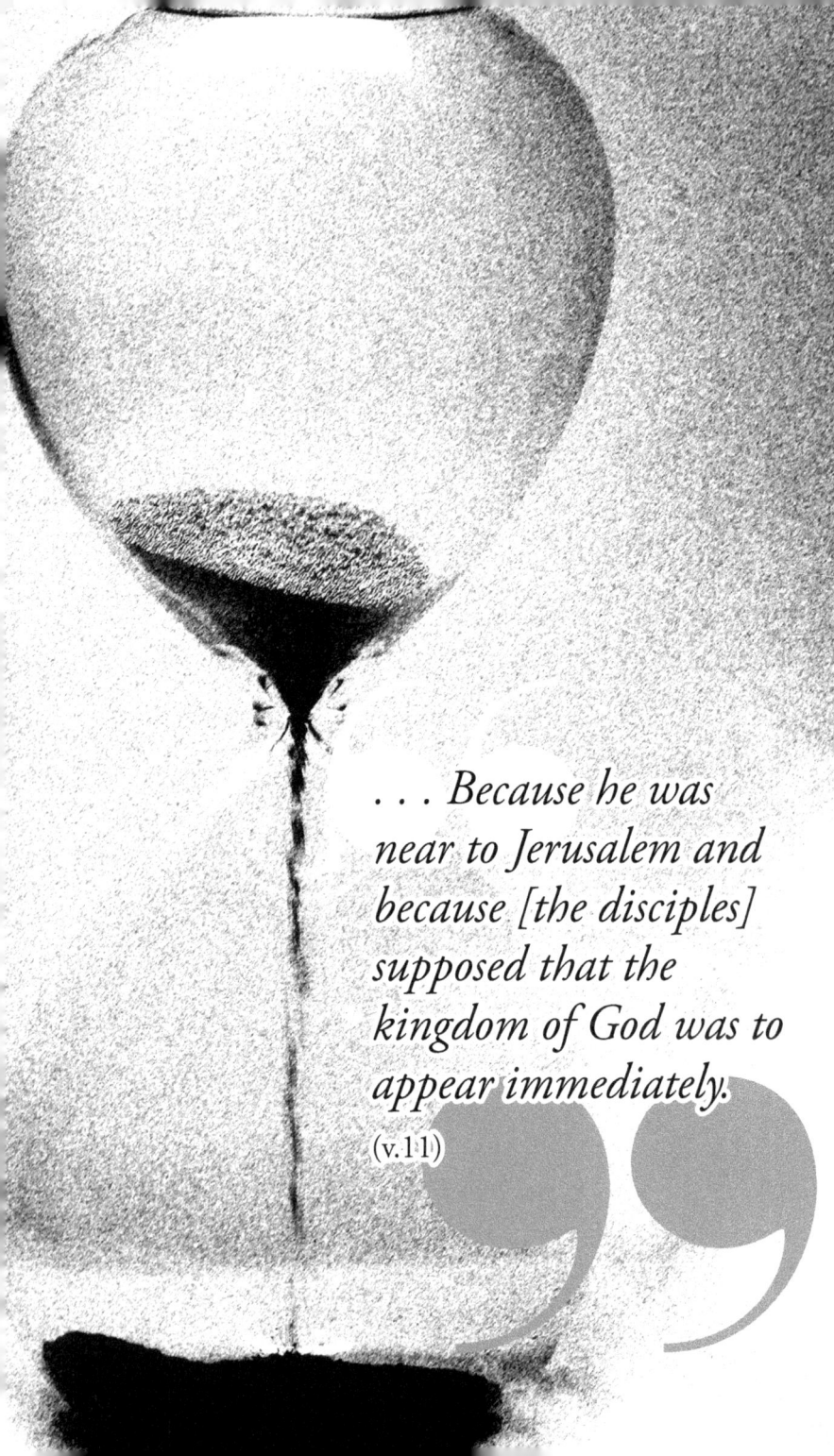

. . . Because he was near to Jerusalem and because [the disciples] supposed that the kingdom of God was to appear immediately.

(v.11)

CHAPTER 2

WHY DID JESUS TELL THIS PARABLE?

The followers of Jesus were quite excited because they finally understood that Jesus was the Son of God, the Messiah. After being with Him for three years, observing His life, and seeing Him do the supernatural, they thought He would perhaps establish His physical Kingdom the following week during Passover.

However, Jesus knew something the disciples did not. In about a week, He would be killed. Jesus's physical Kingdom would NOT be established at this time. With this parable, Jesus wanted to clarify and correct their misconception that His Kingdom would be established immediately. He instructed them that He needed to go away for a while. In the meantime, He had a job for them to do, and when they finished, He would return.

Here is a thought-provoking question:

Where was Jesus when He told this story?

Remember the little man, Zacchaeus, the tax collector who lived in Jericho, about twenty-two miles from Jerusalem? Do you remember the interaction between Jesus and Zacchaeus?

No one knows exactly what Jesus said when He was in Zacchaeus's home. Still, Zacchaeus had a face-to-face encounter that radically altered everything in his life. Because of it, he showed the immediate fruits of his repentance: He asked forgiveness of those he had wronged and returned four times the money he had stolen from them. That is a strong indicator of a changed life!

Now, here is what is interesting:

As Jesus walked out the door of Zacchaeus's home, He said something to His disciples that reminded them of *His* mission. This word would serve as a segue to explain *their* mission.

"For the Son of Man came to seek and to save the lost."[2]

---

2   Luke 19:10

Here it is. Jesus, the Son of Man, *came to seek and to save the lost.*

Jesus declared His purpose for coming to this earth, stating that He wasn't here just to do nice things or show us how to live good lives. He was here to search for and bring salvation to lost people.

Just as they heard these things, Jesus told the Parable of the Ten Minas.

Take a few minutes to read it for yourself in Luke 19:11–27. Jesus has one week left before He will be slaughtered in Jerusalem. Now is the time to finish hammering into the hearts of His followers His most important material. So He says, "I have come to seek and to save the lost." Standing now in the doorway of the transformed Zacchaeus, He looks at His disciples and, in essence, states, "I am now passing the baton to you. As I was, so are you now in the world.[3] I want you to continue with my mission of seeking and saving the lost." This "Great Commission" is a prelude to what the disciples will hear right before Jesus goes into Heaven.

Isn't it interesting that Jesus continued on mission a week before His death and was still looking for the lost? Doesn't it amaze you even more that He remained active

---

3   1 John 4:17

with His call to seek and save right up to and including the time of the cross when He told the thief next to Him that the thief would join him in Paradise?

Jesus walks out the door of Zacchaeus's home and tells His followers the Parable of the Ten Minas: a story to help them understand the "one job" He is commissioning them to do.

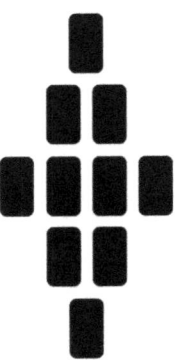

A nobleman went into a far country to receive for himself a kingdom and then return.

(v.12)

CHAPTER 3

THE NOBLEMAN

There are a few things I will help define to understand this parable better.

The Nobleman. Jesus refers to Himself as a nobleman who came from a far country. That country was Heaven.

Why did Jesus have to leave this earth? Jesus said that He had to receive for Himself a Kingdom, and then, after He received the Kingdom, He would return.

Here are a few reasons Jesus came to earth originally:

- To seek and save the lost.
- To take away the sins of the world.
- To destroy the works of the devil.

- To reconcile us to His Father.
- To establish His kingdom in our hearts.

He fulfilled His part of the mission. He came to take away the sins of the world. That was His job. Although Jesus fulfilled **His** mission, His servants must complete **their** mission. When they do so, Jesus will come back.

At this point, the parable becomes personal. It is where you will begin to understand that for Jesus to receive His Kingdom fully, He needs you to do your job.

Although Jesus fulfilled *His* mission, His servants must complete *their* mission.

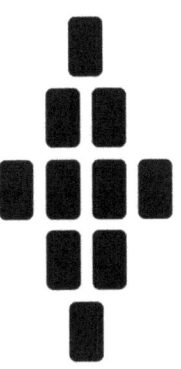

Calling ten of his servants, he gave them ten minas.

(v.13)

CHAPTER 4

THE TEN SERVANTS

Who are the servants? "They are people who willingly live under Christ's authority as His devoted followers. It is someone who belongs to another, a bond slave, without any ownership rights. The essential meaning of servant is belonging—and belonging to Christ is life's highest honor."[4]

So the nobleman (Jesus) calls ten of his servants and distributes ten minas.

Each servant received one mina. All the servants were equally responsible for what the nobleman gave them, and their responsibility could not be transferred to someone else. Remember that some call themselves servants but

---

4   Gary Hill, *The Discovery Bible.* Entry: G1401, H.E.L.P.S Ministries, thediscoverybible.com.

don't do what their master tells them.[5] These are the unfaithful servants.

When reading about the ten minas, most people immediately think of the Parable of the Talents in Matthew 25.[6] They are definitely related and work together, yet they are different. For example, in the Parable of the Talents, Jesus gave to one servant five talents, to another two, and to another just one—each according to his ability. Yet, in the Parable of the Ten Minas, each servant receives the same amount. A bit later, you will understand how these two parables work hand in hand.

Now, it is time to unravel the meaning of the Mina!

All the servants were equally responsible for what the nobleman gave them, and their responsibility could not be transferred to someone else.

---

5   Luke 6:46

6   Matthew 25:14–30

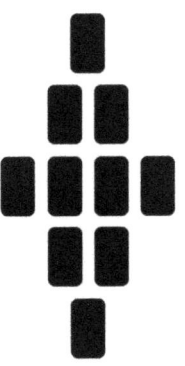

. . . He gave them **ten minas.**

(v.13)

CHAPTER 5

THE MYSTERY OF THE MINA

Before discovering the significance of the Mina, we need to know what a mina is. Historically, a mina was a silver ingot weighing sixteen ounces or one pound. This silver ingot was worth about three months' wages in the first century.

What does the Mina represent in this parable?

This is important because once you know the spiritual meaning of the Mina, you will understand more clearly the one job Jesus expects you to do.

Let me share a few Scriptures from the Bible that have helped me interpret the significance of the Mina.

1.   What was Jesus doing right before He told this story? He was bringing salvation to the house of a sinner. That encounter with Zacchaeus inspired Him to tell the story of the Ten Minas.

2. Jesus said, "As the Father has sent me, even so, I am sending you."[7] Jesus's mission was to seek and to save the lost.

3. A couple of months later, as Jesus was about to ascend into "a far country," He said, "All authority in heaven and on earth has been given to me. Therefore, go and *make disciples* of all nations, *baptizing* them in the name of the Father, the Son, and the Holy Spirit, *teaching* them to observe all that I have commanded you. And behold, I am with you always, to the end of the age" (emphasis added).[8] Does this sound like what the nobleman said to the ten servants when he gave them the ten minas? He told them to go and do business with the mina while he was gone.

4. On the same mountain, another disciple heard Jesus say, "Go into all the world and *proclaim the gospel* to the whole creation. Whoever believes and is baptized will be saved, but whoever does not believe will be condemned."[9] Jesus was about to go to a faraway country and told them **again** what He wanted them to do when He was gone.

---

7 John 20:21
8 Matthew 28:18–20, emphasis mine
9 Mark 16:15–16

5.   Later in the story, the servants present what they had gained in their business to the nobleman and say, "Lord, your mina has gained . . . ." This statement indicates that the Mina is not ours (like talents are not ours) but belongs to the Lord. What did Jesus give all His followers equally that belonged to Himself?

6.   Jesus says, "And this *Gospel of the kingdom* will be proclaimed throughout the whole world as a testimony to all nations, and then the end will come."[10] So Jesus will return when He receives His kingdom. When is that? When the Gospel is proclaimed throughout the whole world.

My conclusion from the points above is that the Mina represents the **GOSPEL MESSAGE**.

Having consulted dozens of biblical commentaries, I have found that many confuse the Parable of the Ten Minas with the Parable of the Talents. Others don't even offer an interpretation of the Mina or its significance. However, I have discovered others who also conclude that the Mina represents the Gospel message. Here are a couple of them.

1.   Charles Spurgeon says of the servant and the Mina: "They were his confidants and trustees. His eye was

---

10   Matthew 24:14

not watching them, for he had gone into a far country and trusted them to be a law unto themselves. They were not to render a daily account but to be left alone until he returned. Now that is just how the Master has treated us: he has put us **in trust with the Gospel** and relies upon our honor."[11]

2.   G. Campbell Morgan said, "We may not have ten talents, but that is another matter. The pound [Mina] is something other than a gift. The pound is a deposit, and it is the **Gospel** of the Grace of God. We are witnesses to that Gospel."[12]

3.   William Taylor states, "For this purpose, he has given each a pound, the common blessing of the **gospel** and its opportunities. The talents differed for each servant, but the pound was the same for all."[13]

The Mina Represents the Gospel Message

The Gospel Message! What power there is in the Mina! The power of God unto salvation! Explosive power!

---

11   C. H. Spurgeon, *Our Lord's Parables* (Passmore & Edinburgh: London, 1904), p. 245.

12   G. Campbell Morgan, *The Parables and Metaphors of Our Lord* (Marshall, Morgan and Scott, 1943), p. 247.

13   William M. Taylor, *The Parables of Our Savior* (Kregel Publications, Grand Rapids, MI, 1975) p. 437.

Transforming power! Power to save a soul from eternal fires! Power to free us from the devil and break the chains of sin! Power to forgive the sins from the book of our lives! Power to declare us not guilty before God the Father! Power to make us holy and acceptable before God! Power to open the doors to Heaven! Power to make you a son or daughter of the Father! Power to reconcile you to God and become His friend!

The Gospel Message! Jesus took our place. The innocent for the guilty. The righteous for the unrighteous. The clean for the filthy. Jesus drank the cup of wrath and judgment, so we don't have to!

The Gospel Message is just that. It is a message freely proclaimed, offered, and received. You are saved by grace through faith; it is not your own doing but a gift from God.[14]

Understanding the Mina as the Gospel Message not only helps you understand the meaning of the parable, but it also defines your mission as a servant of Jesus. It describes the one job He gave you to do in His absence.

---

14   Ephesians 2:8

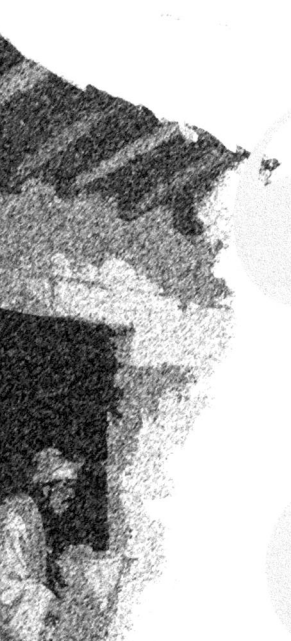

Engage in business until I come.

(v.13)

CHAPTER 6

DO BUSINESS

The nobleman in the Parable of the Ten Minas left no doubt about his expectations for his servants! They were to take the mina and engage in business until he returned.

Doing business implies doing something profitable or beneficial. Jesus (your Nobleman) gave you a powerful Mina, and you are to put it to work—bartering, trading, negotiating, investing, and multiplying that Gospel Message to the best of your abilities.

The exciting thing is that the Holy Spirit has equipped you with everything you need to do business with the Mina.

Check out how the Parable of the Talents works with the Parable of the Ten Minas. The Spirit of God gives "talents" to every servant, each according to the servant's ability and as the Spirit Himself wills.[15]

Both the mina and the talent were ancient units of weight. A talent in historical times was a literal amount of silver equivalent to sixty pounds. In these two parables, however, these units of weight are given a spiritual significance: the Mina being the Gospel message and the Talents being our giftings and abilities.

One **Mina** = 1 silver bar weighing one pound.

One **Talent** = 60 silver bars weighing 60 pounds.

Two **Talents** = 120 silver bars weighing 120 pounds.

Five **Talents** = 300 silver bars weighing 300 pounds.

Therefore, even if you are a one-talent servant, God has given you an abundance of giftings to do business with the Gospel! You have no excuse not to do business. You have so much!

The talent in the Matthew 25 parable represents what God has given you specifically and uniquely as his servant. No one else has exactly what you have. You are the only one who can do the work God prepared for you to do.

---

15   Matthew 25:15: "To one he gave five talents, to another two, to another one, to each according to his ability. Then he went away."

These include your abilities, special graces, personality, life opportunities, spiritual gifts, money, health, strength, etc.

So, let's get practical for a few minutes and discuss how we can do business with the Mina.

Here are three ways you can invest the Mina.
1. Invest the Mina in yourself.
2. Share the Mina with the citizens (unbelievers) of this world.
3. Apply the Mina by discipling God's servants.

1. Invest the Mina in yourself.

I will say that again. Invest the Mina in yourself! The Gospel *has* to be applied to your own life first. You must allow the Gospel to affect you entirely, transform your life, or you risk being an unfaithful, wicked servant. Dreadful is the case of the "religious person" or the "Pharisees" who has a form of godliness but denies the power of what Jesus did for them on the cross by not allowing the Gospel to transform their own lives.

It saddens me to think of the many people within our churches who are mere "professors" only. They profess or say they are Christians and claim the name of Christian, but they have not been truly born again. They have no new nature, no indwelling Spirit of God, no fragrance of

Christ, and no fruits of repentance. They do no business with the Mina because they have no heart or desire to do so. A motivation to evangelize, live holy, and disciple others only comes from a new nature.

Philip Ryken says, "Here are some ways we can put the gospel to work. We do it by growing in our Christian lives through repentance, prayer, and daily dependence on the Holy Spirit. We do it by trusting God to meet our needs and guide our decisions."[16]

Scores of people are handed the Mina every week in church and do nothing to apply it to their lives. You do *not* want to be that person! Make sure you invest the Mina in yourself.

2. Share the Mina with the citizens of this world.

Jesus stated that as the Father sent Him, He was sending us to be a light shining in the darkness, the salt of the earth, to go into all the world. How shall the lost call upon the name of the Lord if they have no one to tell them of Him? We are Christ's ambassadors/representatives, imploring the citizens and urging them to reconcile and make peace with God.

---

16   Christian theologian and president of Wheaton College, Philip Graham Ryken, *Gospel of Luke: Volume 2, Reformed Expository Commentary* (P&R Publishing, 2009).

That is doing business with the Mina.

No age or location can limit your business. My mother-in-law is in an assisted living home. Although she cannot get out much, she gives to missions—investing her money in others who can be on the front lines. She prays for those living down her hallway and intercedes for the salvation of her family and friends. That is effective Mina business!

Another example of Mina business comes from a young woman from Mexico. She received a literal pound of silver worth $500. When she shared the Mina message with her pastor, he asked her to share it with the church. Inspired, the people formed an evangelism team. This team went to the streets of their town and shared the Gospel. As people repented and decided to follow Jesus, this woman and the evangelism team invited them to the coffee house at the church to help them grow in their new faith. Soon, they outgrew their old place and had to add on. They renamed the new coffee shop "Café La Mina" (The Mina Coffee Shop). Then she melted down the silver bar, made a mold of a miniature Mina the size of your thumbnail, and put little Minas on the chains of necklaces and bracelets. Now she sells them, giving the profits to missions! She is doing a great job at the Mina business!

3. Apply the Mina through discipling God's servants.

The Great Commission is two-fold: proclaiming the Mina (Gospel) and discipling those who accept the Gospel. Discipleship, in its truest sense, is not "attending a class." It is taking a fellow servant alongside you and saying, "Follow me as I follow Christ. Do as I do." (See how important it is to consume and integrate the Mina into your life first?) Let the new believer hear you pray. Allow them to shadow you as you share the Gospel with someone. Study the Scripture together. Ask, "What is the Lord speaking to you during your devotional time?" Hold them accountable. Teach them to obey all the things that Christ taught us. That also helps others do business with the Mina.

Jesus does not tell His servants **how** to do business and make a profit with His message. I think it is a good thing He didn't! Suppose He gave us a methodology by saying we all needed to stand on a red box on the street corner and proclaim the Gospel. In that case, we may reel back and say, "Well, I am not so sure about that!" The "how" is what the Holy Spirit will reveal to you according to your gifts and talents. Remember, there may be a thousand different methods, but there is only one Message. God gives you all the equipment you need, and then it is up to you to discover, with the help of the Holy Spirit, the "how."

Many people are involved in Mina projects that meet people's physical needs. "We also put the gospel to work by serving people in need, showing the love and mercy of Christ to people who are lonely, sick, homeless, grieving, and afraid. Then, we put the gospel to work by loving our families with the love of Jesus and sharing our faith with our friends. Putting the gospel to work by investing in missionary work, praying, giving, sending, and going to The Nations with the good news about Jesus Christ."[17]

Remember this: you can do many "good things" in the world, which are essential, but the Red Cross does many good things. Unbelievers feed the hungry and dig wells for fresh water. One doesn't need to be a follower of Christ to do that. But there is something only *you* can give the world that no one else can: **the Gospel Message**. Practice the former without neglecting the latter.

The story of the Sower will also help you understand your business with the Mina.

Keep in mind, the Mina is not yours but God's. In the Parable of the Sower, the seed is the Gospel—the same as the Mina. Just like when you plant the seed into people's lives and it falls on hearts with differing levels of soil

---

17   Ryken, *Gospel of Luke.*

readiness, so too when you offer the Mina message, the responses will be different.

Remember: You do not determine what kind of heart the seed/mina (the Gospel) falls into.

1. Some people will have a hard heart and won't understand the message, and the Devil will immediately steal the Mina you offer.

2. Some will hear the Mina message and receive it with joy. Yet when tough times come, they will fall away because the Gospel didn't take root.

3. Others hear the word of the Mina, but they love the world more. Their love for riches and pleasure steals the Mina, yielding no return on investment.

4. Then there is a group of people with open hearts, and when the Mina is offered to them, they understand it, willingly accept it, and it produces abundant return.

I sure hope you didn't skip over that story. "Yeah, I already know that one." If you skipped those four points, go back and read them.

Here are some things I've learned about sowing or "investing" the Mina.

1. Just as it is our job to scatter seeds, it is our job to offer the Mina.

2. All four hearts hear the Gospel, but only one shows fruit of SALVATION.

3. Not all who raise their hands, come forward at an altar call, or say a sinners' prayer are born again. Be very careful if you are one who "counts decisions for Christ." You don't know what has truly happened in that person's heart. Only God knows. With time, we may see the fruits of repentance. Then, if there is fruit and they continue growing, we will know that the Mina has been accepted and applied to their soul.

Success in your Mina business

The biggest frustration in evangelism and discipleship is the lack of immediate fruit or visible results. We feel unsuccessful if we don't quickly see what we want or expect.

I need to say that again. If you measure your success by rapid results, you will frustrate yourself, get discouraged, and possibly quit the business.

Success in the Mina business is measured differently than success in an earthly business. Your success is measured by your faithfulness in sharing the Gospel, not your immediate visible results.

You are not responsible for the outcome—God is! If you exaggerate external results to look good before your peers, you will dilute the Gospel Message to make it more palatable and less offensive. You will stop talking about sin, judgment, eternity, Hell, the awfulness of the cross, the wrath of God, and repentance. You will fall into encouraging people to repeat a prayer void of repentance if they want a better life and a free ticket to Heaven.

My friend, I am not sure how to tell you this. You do NOT want to be that person on the final day who stands before Jesus and confesses that you manipulated the Mina by mixing it with worthless alloys and stripping it of all its power and worth.

Seriously! The Mina is not to be messed with.

Before I conclude this chapter, I want to help you define your role and responsibility in the Mina business.

There are three roles in ministry.
1.   God's role.
2.   Your role.
3.   The sinner's role.

God's Role

Let's clarify that this business plan is all God's idea from the beginning. Yes, He invited you into a partnership, and you have become a co-laborer with Christ. Yet the idea was His. The message is His. The power comes from Him. He gives the increase. He causes the fruit to ripen. He convicts of sin. He saves the soul. He builds His church.

He advances His kingdom. He writes people's names in the Book of Life when they repent. He does all the heavy lifting. The burden of this Mina business falls on His shoulders. Salvation belongs to God. Therefore, you will be frustrated and unsuccessful if you try to do God's job.

Your Role

We are in partnership with God, and even though our role is "small," it is crucial. Searching through the Scriptures, I discover that our role in this Mina business is very much like the sower's job: planting and watering the Gospel. And sometimes, God even allows us to accompany Him in the harvest.

> I planted, Apollos watered, but God gave the growth. So neither he who plants nor he who waters is anything, but only God who gives the growth. He who plants and he who waters are one, and each will receive his wages according to his labor. For we are God's fellow workers. You are God's field, God's building. (1 Cor. 3:6–9)

He sends us to the highways and byways to compel them to come in. Stick to your job, and you will be a faithful servant. Not only that, you will feel the approval of God upon your life, you will feel useful, you will have a purpose in your life, and you will have something to live for. When the weight of results is off your shoulders and onto God's, you will begin to enjoy the Mina business more than ever.

Sinner's Role

You can bank on God doing His job, and God trusts that you will do your job. Yet the sinners must make their move. They must call upon the name of the Lord. They must recognize they have offended God and repent. Then, their sins will be blotted out, and their guilt will be lifted. But it is their choice. God chooses *not* to do that for them. You *cannot* do that for them. Their role is to repent and believe.

You understand now that your mission in life is to engage in the Mina business. Why is this so important? One reason is for the love of the citizens.

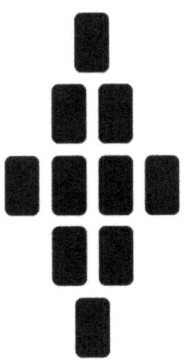

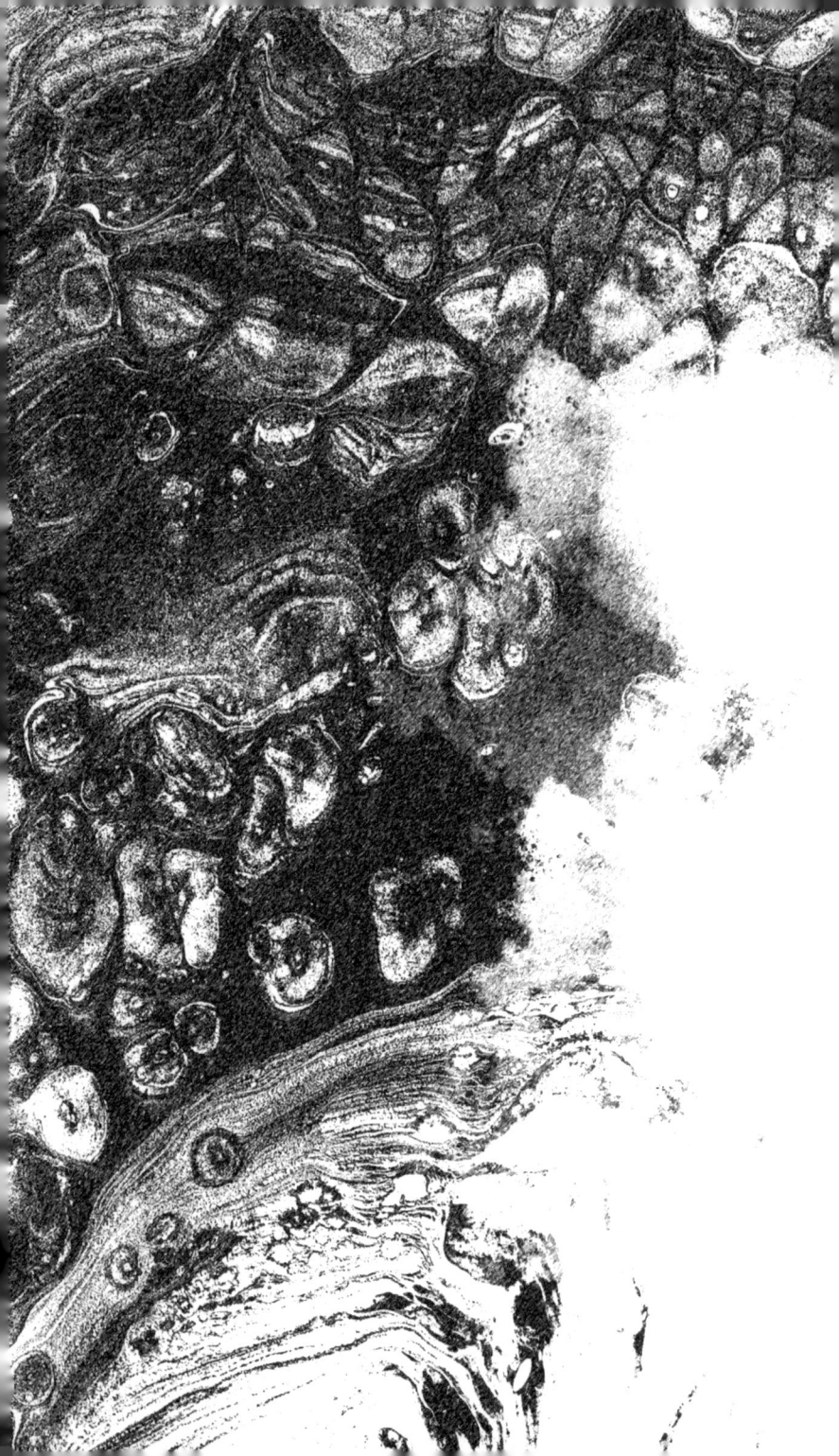

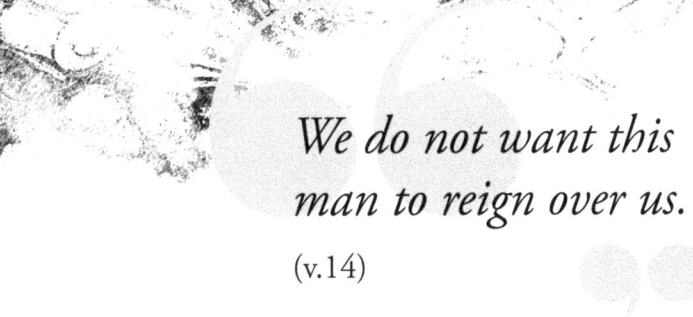

We do not want this man to reign over us.

(v.14)

CHAPTER 7

THE CITIZENS

Who are the citizens? All those who are not Christ's servants.

Jesus refers to the citizens as His enemies, rebels to His kingdom. They did *not* want Jesus to reign over them. They were not willing for Him to be Lord and for Him to direct and guide their lives. They wanted to do things their way and didn't want anyone to tell them what to do. Their philosophy in life would be, "I will do what I want, with whom I want, and when I want."

They are rebels because they were born that way. Original sin is in their human DNA. Their stony hearts cannot submit to God. It is not so much ignorance or lack of knowledge that keeps them from submitting to God's will but simply a hard heart.

Most of your friends and family who have not bent their knees to the Lordship of Jesus are citizens because they choose to be. They refuse to say, "Not my will, but yours be done." Oh, how obstinate and rebellious is a depraved will!

The citizens want their immoral sex, their money, their entertainment, their better jobs, their popularity, their religion, and their way. They do not want God's way.

In your church, there are both servants and citizens. Don't *you* be fooled—even though *they* may be. The citizens are quick to be religious, say a prayer, show their faces in church, sing songs, give money in the offering, and have God on their lips. And yet, their hearts are far from Him. They may believe in God but do not tremble, even though the demons do.

God has sent you to do business with the Mina for the sake of the citizens. He wants you to use all the talents you have been assigned with the hope of turning some from darkness to light.

Knowing what Jesus suffered on the Cross for their sake should be motivation enough to engage in business among them.

Also, knowing what happens to the citizens on Judgment Day should motivate you to do business with them! (See Luke 19:27)

The historic part of the story has now ended. We will now move forward into the future when the Nobleman returns in power and glory.

When he returned, having received his kingdom . . .

(v.15)

CHAPTER 8

JESUS RETURNS

The Nobleman is back!

He will send His angels with a loud trumpet call, and they will gather His elect from the four winds—from one end of Heaven to the other. The Gospel has reached the ends of the earth, the number of the Gentiles is completed, and the elect are saved. The Nobleman has finally received His kingdom, and the Father stood up and shut the door of mercy and salvation.

Life as we know it will be over. Heaven and earth are burned up. Our Mina business will have come to a close. Your eternal destination will have already been determined. Nothing that matters to you today will matter on that day except what you did for Him.

It is at this point in the parable that you find yourself. We are all there. We are standing before the Nobleman, Jesus, giving an account. We have all been warned that this would happen. We all knew what our job was. Jesus talked about this day in so many of His teachings. This truth should come as no surprise.

For the genuine servant of Christ, there is no fear of being cast away into outer darkness. Salvation was not earned. We did not work for it; it is not of ourselves but rather a gift from God. However, our *reward* and position in Heaven are based on our work with the Mina. The more you do business with the Mina, the more reward you will receive.

Now, it's time to appear before the Nobleman and give an account of how we've used His Mina.

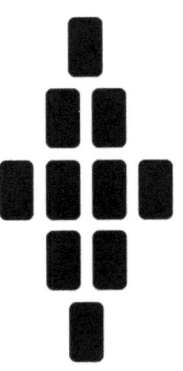

The first came before him,
saying, 'Lord, your mina
has made ten minas more.'
(v.16)

CHAPTER 9

THE FIRST SERVANT

Well, this is the moment of truth! All of your life culminates in this moment. Now you understand what Jesus meant when He told you to store your treasures in Heaven and not on earth. It makes sense why we were to set our mind on things above and not on things of the world. Also, whatever we do, we do for Him and not for men, knowing that we will receive an inheritance as our reward because we have served Christ.

Here, God is not asking us what church or religion we belong to. It will not matter if you are an Arminian or Calvinist or prefer to worship God by clapping and raising your arms or kneeling in quietness before him. What will matter is how many Minas you have on that day to give back to God.

Note the servant's words: "Lord, *your* Mina has made ten Minas more" (emphasis added). That is a 1,000% return! The servant was acutely aware of whose Mina he was holding. It is the Lord's Mina, not the servant's. **The first servant was the caretaker and investor, but the nobleman made the original investment.** The power of multiplication lies within the Mina. Mina produces Mina. The Mina multiplies itself. You can never run out.

Perhaps the first servant didn't know how much the Lord's Mina produced until the nobleman arrived. The first servant did the work; the treasure was invested wisely, and the results of his work were not counted up until that day.

Observe how the Lord responds: "Well done, good servant!"

Blessed are you among the sons of men, Mr. First Servant. Did you hear what the Lord said to you? Did you notice the exclamation point at the end of "Well done, good servant!"? (Would this not be reward enough?)

Jesus's words of affirmation, "Well done," are reserved for those who did their job and present the Mina multiplied. Attending church, having a devotional time, and being a good neighbor are essential. Nevertheless, if you want to hear "Well done," you must arrive with more than just the one Mina you were given. May it be your goal to hear those monumental words when you see Jesus face to face.

The story continues, "Because you have been faithful

in a very little . . . ." The first servant was praised for his *faithfulness*, not for the number of Minas he gave back to Jesus. Jesus asks little of us. It is just a little. Just give away a silver bar. It is not that difficult. If someone doesn't want it, offer it to someone else. God is not asking you to do *His* job. Just share the Message. He who is faithful in little will be given much.

Then the nobleman says, "You shall have authority over ten cities."

The first servant presents ten minas and reigns with Jesus over ten cities. The more you work now, the more you will receive that day. The more you present to Jesus that day, the more He will give you in return. Jesus pays very high dividends for the "little" that we have done.

Your faithfulness in the Mina business now will grant you authority in Heaven and give you the privilege to reign with Him. I don't know what all that means, but even though that truth may be shrouded in some mystery, it still sounds good!

In this world, you will possibly see little reward for your labor. God's grace allows us only to get a glimpse of a few results on earth, for not many egos could handle great visible success. In your Mina business, you will only see a small percentage of the good you are doing. Your eternal treasures will remain invisible while on earth. Therefore, let us keep working and anticipate that final day when we will receive our reward.

It is interesting to note that no two servants will get the same reward. Some may have had more talents or could have worked harder. What seems clear is that we are determining right now the amount of reward we will receive on that day.

The second servant now enters the room.

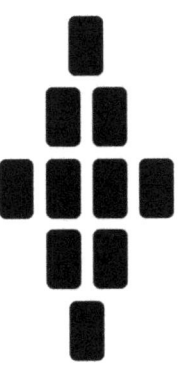

'Lord, your mina has made five minas.'

(v.18)

CHAPTER 10

THE SECOND SERVANT

"Next. Your name, please?"

"I'm the second servant."

"Ok. What do you have for me today?"

"Lord, your Mina has made five Minas." (That is a 500% increase!)

There will be a day when we will stand before Jesus individually.

Even though the story does not record that the second servant heard, "Well done," he did get five cities for his return of five minas, so we can assume the nobleman was pleased. The second servant was not compared to the first servant. So whether you present many Minas or just a few to the Nobleman, faithfulness to your job is what He rewards.

Not all faithful servants have the same success. Many in the Bible did not have many visible converts yet were considered faithful.

God told Jeremiah, "So you shall speak all these words to them, but they will not listen to you. You shall call to them, but they will not answer you" (Jer. 7:27). He had God's heart and the Message from God. Yet, he wept most of his ministry as the people would not turn to the Lord. Yet Jeremiah was a faithful servant.

Noah was a preacher of righteousness, and yet it was said of his generation, "The Lord saw that the wickedness of man was great in the earth and that every intention of the thoughts of his heart was only evil continually" (Gen. 6:5). Verses 11 and 12 say, "Now the earth was corrupt in God's sight, and the earth was filled with violence. And God saw the earth, and behold, it was corrupt, for all flesh had corrupted their way on the earth." However, "Noah found favor in the eyes of the Lord" (verse 8).

God only rescued eight people from death out of the whole world. No one else responded to Noah's warning. Yet Noah was deemed faithful.

Jesus preached for over three years, and only a few were there to say goodbye to Him at His ascension. Yet He was faithful.

You can bank on the fact that your faithfulness and Mina business will have a reward. You can trust that Jesus will be generous.

In these first two accounts, all is wonderful, as we see rewards given to faithful servants. Yet it is not so with the next servant.

Then another came, saying, 'Lord, here is your mina, which I kept laid away in a handkerchief; for I was afraid of you, because you are a severe man. You take what you did not deposit and reap what you did not sow.'

(v.20-21)

CHAPTER 11

THE THIRD SERVANT

Jesus spends a lot of time on the third servant. The nobleman's interaction with the first two servants contains just two verses each. This third one, however, gets six.

Why is so much time dedicated to a wicked, graceless servant?

Is it because that is where much of the professing Church is today?

According to statistics, Christianity is the world's largest religion, with adherents estimated to number 2.5 billion people. This statistic represents roughly one-third of the global population. If they were all faithful servants, then statistically, we would only have to share the Gospel with about two other people each; our job would be done!

A great many professing Christians are unfaithful servants. They neglect or disregard what they have been told to do. Walking the wide path seems easier and involves less sacrifice. Neither the citizens nor the unfaithful servant did any striving to enter the narrow gate. Oh, that they would have!

So, let's talk about this massive group of professing Christians.

Woe to you who say you are Christians but do not obey your Lord! You were offered the Mina many times but never took it and applied it to yourself. You were so close to salvation but chose not to receive it. Your mind knew the message, but you rejected it. Did not what Christ did for you on the cross move you to turn away from your sins? Did not the warnings of a hell burning with fire and brimstone strike the fear of God in you and rattle you to the core? Did you really think you could do many things in His name while continuing to sin and expect the door of Heaven to be open for you?

"Lord, Lord, open to us!"

Lord? *Then* you will call him Lord? God will not acknowledge you—just as you did not acknowledge Him. Woe to you professing Christian when you hear the dreadful words, "Depart from me" spoken by the One who desired to be your Savior. The Lamb of God could have taken away your sins, but you were unwilling. Because of your choices, the wrath of the Lamb sends you away to outer darkness, where there will be weeping and gnashing of teeth. You will see the faithful servants enter Heaven, along with Abraham, Isaac, and Jacob, but you will be excluded.

Let's get back to the story.

When the nobleman called him, the third servant responded, "Lord, here is your mina." (That is a 0% profit!)

What? You are giving the Mina back to Jesus? This is the only message that could save your soul, and you wrapped it up and forgot about it?

"Be appalled, O heavens, at this; be shocked, be utterly desolate," declares the Lord.[18] You spurned the gift of God and insulted Him by trying to give the Gospel back?

"Just think how much worse the punishment will be for those who have trampled on the Son of God, and have treated the blood of the covenant, which made us holy, as if it were common and unholy, and have insulted and disdained the Holy Spirit who brings God's mercy to us" (Heb. 10:29, NLT).

---

18   See Jeremiah 2:12

The excuses that at one time eased the third servant's conscience do the servant no good on his day of judgment. He hid the Mina with the flimsy excuse that he was afraid. This servant wasn't timid. He was lazy and wicked. Inactivity and laziness were his excuses. If he had enough energy to wrap the Mina in a napkin, hide it, and go about his worldly business, surely he could have had some energy to do business with the Gospel. Yet he said he was afraid. If he had the fear of God, then why didn't he invest the Mina?

The third servant said he was afraid and accused the nobleman of being severe because He reaps where He did not sow.

Interestingly, Jesus did not correct this assessment. "You knew I was a severe man . . . ." All we have to do is read the last verse of the parable, and we can agree that God is severe when He slaughters His enemies. Note then the kindness and the severity of God: severity toward those who have fallen, but God's kindness to his servants, provided they continue to obey Him. Otherwise, they, too, will be cut off.[19] If you have trouble believing God is severe, just look at the cross and see the severity of God poured out on His Son. God is both severe and kind. You choose now how you want Him to be towards you in the end.

---

19   See Romans 11:22.

The third servant accuses God of reaping where He did not sow. In other words, God does whatever He pleases.

Of course, God does whatever He pleases!

Yet it pleased the Father to send Jesus to earth. To sacrifice Him and crush Him. It pleased the Father that Jesus would bear the sins and guilt of all His enemies. It pleased the Father for his Son to drink from the cup of His wrath so that you wouldn't have to. It pleased the Son to taste death for you so you could live. It pleased the Son to take the keys of death and the grave so you can live forever.

Yes! God does as He pleases. And I am so grateful He does!

'I will condemn you with your own words, you wicked servant! You knew that I was a severe man, taking what I did not deposit and reaping what I did not sow? Why then did you not put my money in the bank, and at my coming, I might have collected it with interest? . . Take the mina from him.'

(v.22-24)

CHAPTER 12

THE THIRD SERVANT, PART II

The nobleman pronounces the verdict, and the third servant is called wicked. In the New Testament, the word "wicked" is also translated as evil, bad, malicious, and slothful.[20] He proved his wickedness by refusing the instructions of his master. Instead of using the pound of silver to turn a profit, the Mina that he had been given was taken out of circulation and hidden in a handkerchief.[21]

---

20   Biblehub.com/greek/Strongs 4190.htm

21   Joel B. Green, *The Gospel of Luke: The New International Commentary on the New Testament* (Wm B. Eerdmans Publishing Company; Grand Rapids, MI),

It wasn't even put in the bank to make interest. The third servant did not believe in the value and power of the Mina. When the business is so urgent and the commission so clear, his silence and inactivity are inexcusable.[22]

In the financial world, there are two ways of making money: active and passive. "Active income is defined as any income generated that requires your constant time and energy."[23] Examples include hourly wages, salary, and sales commissions. If you don't put in any effort, you don't get any return. This is you pushing up your sleeves, pulling on your boots, getting dirty, and doing the work.

"Passive income is any money earned in a manner that does not require too much effort."[24] Some examples are bank interest, stocks, bonds, and rental properties. You make the initial investment and then your money works for you while you do something else or even sleep.

The *least* this servant could have done was deposit the silver bar in the bank and allow it to earn interest. Having done that, on the day of reckoning, he would

---

1997.

22   Fred B. Craddock, *Interpretation: A Bible Commentary for Teaching and Preaching* (Westminster John Knox Press; Louisville, KY, 1990).

23   https://www.financialsamurai.com/difference-between-active-income-and-passive-income/

24   https://corporatefinanceinstitute.com/resources/accounting/passive-income/

not have appeared before the master empty-handed. The nobleman's expectation was for the servant to multiply the Mina, which takes an active investment of their time and energy. When it comes to doing business with the Gospel, the more active we are in that work, the more pleased the master will be with the results. Some can do more and others less, but just do something! Jesus has called you to put the Mina to work. The third servant was given the task of investing the Mina in some way. Yet, he chose to cave in to fear, laziness, or whatever made him hide the Mina in a handkerchief.

It would be safe to say this did not make the nobleman happy!

"Take the mina from him . . ."

This statement would be a most horrendous thing to hear. Salvation is in your hands, and because of negligence, unbelief, and laziness, it is ripped away from you. The religious, false, and unfaithful servants that hid the Mina will discover in the end that it would have been better had they never been born. I don't think the servant took the time to understand what he possessed!

The nobleman will now condemn the third servant with his own words. The unfaithful servant does not perish on the last day because of a lack of knowledge: "You knew I was severe . . ." The wicked servant by default chose the severity of God and is not even allowed to return the Mina. The nobleman has it taken away from him. Jesus takes it *away from him*! "But from the one who has not, even what he has will be taken away."

You have no hope if God takes the Mina or the Gospel Message from you. I do not believe this servant "lost his salvation." Salvation was offered to him, just as it was to the other servants, but the wicked servant chose not to apply it to himself or do anything with it. He did not value it or believe in it. Therefore, the nobleman removed it from him. He was not a faithful born-again servant. Had the third servant been a genuine servant, he would have been like Zacchaeus and showed some gratitude and fruit of repentance. He would have been obedient to the nobleman.

"The Lord is a harsh taskmaster to the idle servant alone and that because the idle servant has not their Lord's business in his heart. Those who make their Lord's interest their own find that their duty becomes a joyful service."[25]

It did not go well for the third servant. Ultimately, he was no better off than the citizens.

---

25   Norval Geldenhuys, *Commentary on the Gospel of Luke* (Wm B. Eerdmans Publishing Company, Grand Rapids, MI, 1960).

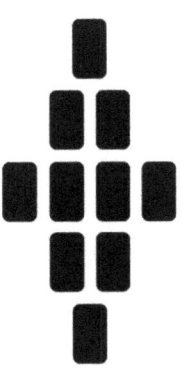

But as for these enemies of mine, who did not want me to reign over them, bring them here and slaughter them before me.

(v.27)

CHAPTER 13

SLAUGHTER THEM BEFORE ME

Jesus always knew how the story would end. We did not. Therefore, He saw fit to warn His servants through this parable about the tragic end for His enemies.

Perhaps He warned His listeners so they could feel the urgency in their hearts to be about their Father's business. When they were being persecuted, rejected, and screamed at—they could look His enemies in the eyes, knowing full well their end. And then, with God's compassion pouring through His servants, they could urge those enemies to reconcile with God.

Remember, God is not willing that any be slaughtered.

God so loved the world that whoever believes, will not be slaughtered.

From the beginning of time, God has desired that He be our God and that we be His people.

He wants a relationship, not a slaughterhouse.

The mission of the Parable of the Ten Minas is for His servants to share the Message of the Gospel and infiltrate enemy territory.

I like almost everything about the Parable of the Mina. It challenges me, gives me purpose, clarifies my mission, inspires me to be a faithful servant, and gives me hope to hear the "Well done" affirmation. However, verse 27 is not my favorite. And I am confident it was not a favorite thing for Jesus to reveal either.

I am convinced of this.

I am convinced because the truth of verse 27 caused Jesus to set His face resolutely toward Jerusalem and ultimately towards the cross. "I gave My back to those who strike Me, and My cheeks to those who pluck out the beard; I did not cover My face from humiliation and spitting. For the Lord GOD helps Me, Therefore, I am not disgraced; Therefore, I have set My face like flint, And I know that I will not be ashamed."[26]

---

26   Isaiah 50:6-7 (NASB 1995)

Because of the truth of verse 27, Jesus threw himself on the ground among the olive trees and asked the Father to take the cup of wrath from him.

I am confident of this because the whole plan of salvation hinged on Jesus getting on that cross and being slaughtered Himself, for His enemies, and for those who did not want Him to rule over them. He was slaughtered so His enemies could become servants and wouldn't have to be slaughtered.

"Bring them here and slaughter them before me."

What a tragic end for the citizens of this world! To be cast away into outer darkness, where there is weeping and gnashing of teeth. To be tied hand and foot and thrown into the fiery furnace with no Savior to rescue you. To go down to the place with the devil and his angels forever and ever. Oh, the dreadful place where the worm never dies and the fire is never quenched!

I don't pretend to understand God's justice and wrath upon sin. But just one look at the cross tells me this is for real and very serious. If Jesus could say, "Not My will but Yours be done" among the olive trees when the Father refused to remove the cup . . could you not say the same thing and pick up that Mina, unwrap it from the napkin, start a "business," produce a profit, and proclaim that Message as He told you to?

CHAPTER 14

WHO ARE YOU?

In this Parable of the Ten Minas, we see three groups of people.

1. Citizens
2. Unfaithful servants
3. Faithful servants

There are no "neutral" people in this story. You are in one of the three categories. You may say it is not your ministry, or you don't want to participate, but you are already in the game. With which group do you most identify? This is a question worthy of deep reflection and honesty.

Are You a Citizen?

You might believe in God, but you are choosing to practice sin, proving your enmity with God. For a citizen to become a faithful servant, you must go through the door of repentance, confess and turn away from all known sins, and submit to the rule of Christ in your life. Perhaps you said before that you were not interested in letting Jesus tell you what to do, but now, by faith, you want to change your mind. You want to say, "God, not my will, but Your will be done in my life." You can begin your life as a servant with that heart and attitude.

Are You an Unfaithful Servant?

You profess with your mouth that you are a Christian. Still, with a casual observation of your life, it is quickly discovered that there is no Mina business, no holiness of heart and life—much lip service, but no fruits of the Spirit. You, my friend, can also do an about-face and become a faithful servant by repenting and submitting your life and will to Christ. Beginning immediately, you can become obedient to your mission in life: doing business and making a profit with the Mina.

Are You a Faithful Servant?

You have His business up and running. Yet most faithful servants want to grow, do more, be better, be more intentional, and strive to get the Gospel out in every way possible. You desire with all your heart to hear the words,

"Well done!" A prayer of commitment to ramp up your business is in order.

If this is you, and you deeply desire to be a faithful servant, I want to share with you four things I have learned in ministry that will serve as a foundation as you work for the Lord. As you put these four things into practice, they will also guarantee the power of God working through you.

CHAPTER 15

ESSENTIAL TOOLS

No one likes to feel ineffective. If we are true servants, we want to be faithful, please God, see results, and not just spin our wheels.

After many years of ministry, I have learned four essential elements for success in Mina business.

1. Understand the Gospel Message.

A most horrendous thing has happened. As I read books from the eighteenth and nineteenth centuries, I see a pattern in every generation: Satan infiltrates the Church and dilutes the Gospel message, stripping it of its power. Diminishing, modifying, or changing the message handed down to us from Jesus and the apostles spits in the face of the Father, the Author of Salvation.

I know I will stand before God to give an account of my message. And so will you. Woe to anyone who modifies it! May you fear and tremble if you change it to make it more palatable to the sinners.

The Gospel Message has so much power, and learning to share it is essential if you want to see God's power move through you.

The Gospel is the power of God for salvation.[27] Understand what the message contains. Apply it to your life. Study it. Live it. Go deep with it. The Gospel is infinite. You cannot reach the end of its height, width, breadth, or depth.[28]

The Gospel Message is divided into four columns:

1. **Our Problem.** We all have sinned by breaking God's commandments.
2. **The Consequence.** We will all die, be judged by God, and our eternal destination determined as either Heaven or Hell.
3. **The Solution.** Jesus Christ paid for our sins and offered us a pardon, forgiveness, and a relationship with Him.
4. **Our Response.** When we repent and place our faith in Christ, Who paid it all, He does the work of salvation in our lives.

---

27   Romans 1:16

28   Read the Bible to understand the Gospel. Read my book, *The Power of the Gospel*, to get an in-depth study of the message of the Mina.

Our Problem

When the rich young ruler asked Jesus what he must do to inherit eternal life, Jesus did not tell him to say the "Sinner's Prayer" or to accept Him as His personal Lord and Savior. Instead, He asked him if he had kept the Ten Commandments.

The rules have not changed since the Garden of Eden: Obey God and live. Disobey God and die. God has rules for being accepted into a relationship with Himself and for having the hope of living in God's home in the future. You don't make the rules. God does.

The young ruler thought he had followed God's rules. Yet he went away sad when He realized he didn't measure up. He was offered treasure in Heaven if he would have been willing to sell all and follow Jesus. But he was not willing, and that revealed what he truly valued.

The Law, including the Ten Commandments, is like a mirror that shows us the condition of our hearts before a perfect God. Looking into that mirror, you recognize that you are not as good of a person as you thought. The Law then declares you guilty before God, leaving you without excuse. That should make you nervous.

For example, when you are driving down the highway, and you pass a police car on the side of the road using radar, what is your reaction? You check your speed. You step on the brake. You check your rear-view mirror numerous times to see if the officer has pulled out of his parked position and turned on his lights. Your heart races and you become nervous. You know what is about to happen, especially if you know you have broken the law.

In the same way, sinners must recognize their dilemma before seeking a solution. Jesus came for the sick, not the healthy. When you share the Mina, use the Law to help others see their desperate predicament. This opens the door to the power of the Holy Spirit, Who is an expert in convicting people of their sins.[29] They will be disturbed and troubled as they see their problem; which brings us to the second column.

The Consequence

The police pull you over, show you the reading on the radar, and give you a ticket.

In the same way, the Law pulls you over, shows you where you missed the mark, and tells you about the fine. The soul that sins shall surely die.[30] The wages of sin is

---

29   John 16:8

30   Ezekiel 18:20

death.[31] It is determined that man dies once and then the judgment.[32]

You know that if you are found guilty on Judgment Day, the doors of Heaven will be closed to you. You don't like to think about Hell, but now it worries you as you don't see any hope. You know God is forgiving and full of love, but you also know He is just and will punish the lawbreaker. Even though the Law shows you your guilt and makes you aware of your fine, it will not pay it.

When we discuss the consequences of breaking God's Law—death, judgment, Heaven, and Hell—it opens the door to the power of the Holy Spirit to move. As He is an expert in convicting sinners of the judgment to come,[33] the Spirit will show sinners that death is imminent, and they will be judged guilty. They will not only lose out on a relationship and friendship with God now but will be cut off forever in a place called Hell.

These are hard truths, but they *are* truths. Understand the Father's heart. He wants to be your God, and He wants you to be His child. He doesn't want anyone to be cast away. When you are giving away the Mina, if you share the

---

31 Romans 6:23

32 Hebrews 9:27

33 John 16:8

problem and the consequence with the right heart, people should respond like they did in Acts, "Sirs, what must I do to be saved?"[34]

Be faithful in sharing the Problem and the Consequence, and God will prepare the ground for your listeners to receive the solution!

The Solution

The Gospel means Good News. The Problem and the Consequence show us our sickness, the bad news. The last two columns show us the powerful, incredible Good News.

Bad News: You can't erase your sins. You can't cleanse your own heart. You can't make yourself righteous before a holy God to be accepted by Him. You and I are powerless! We are helpless!

"But God shows his love for us in that while we were still sinners, Christ died for us."[35]

Good News: Jesus came to take away the sins of the world. He came to be your substitute, to do what you could not do for yourself. Jesus took your guilt on the cross so you could stand before the Father not guilty. He took

---

34   Acts 16:30

35   Romans 5:8

the punishment so you could be shown mercy. Jesus drank the cup of the wrath of God against sin so you would not have to drink it. He paid the fine you could not pay.

He did this because He loves you. He wants to be your Father and have a relationship with you. He does not want you to perish in your sins. On the cross, He paid for your forgiveness, cleansing, freedom, and adoption. With His resurrection, He proved He is God, has power over death, and is the only one in the world who could rescue you from your plight.

Yet only some in the world receive this wonderful gift of salvation—only those who respond to it.

Our Response

To receive all this Good News, you must repent and believe in the Gospel.[36] Peter told the crowd to "repent and be baptized every one of you in the name of Jesus Christ for the forgiveness of your sins, and you will receive the gift of the Holy Spirit."[37]

Your response to the first three columns of the Gospel Message is to turn from your sin and turn to God. It is to declare "not my will, but Yours be done in my life." It is

---

36   Mark 1:15

37   Acts 2:38

saying that you no longer want to be a rebellious citizen; you change your mind. You want Jesus to reign over your life.

Jesus is serious about you confessing your sins to receive forgiveness. Strive to get the sin out of your life. He says if your right eye causes you to sin, you are to gouge it out. You get the idea. He was serious about paying the price for your sin; you need to be serious about repenting of it.

Much of the Church has stopped preaching repentance, and the result is a Church full of people living in sin with the false hope that they are saved. Most are told, "It's easy. All you have to do is ask forgiveness."

There is nothing easy about salvation. It was not easy for Jesus to go to the cross, and there is nothing easy about plucking out an eye to eliminate the sin in your life. It is not easy when your family rejects you, or you lose your job, and you are perceived as becoming a religious fanatic. Salvation is costly.

The good news about the Gospel message is that Jesus paid the price and offers us salvation as a gift, by grace. Our part is to turn from our sin and turn to Him.

That above is a short synopsis of the power-filled Gospel Message that you can share with others.

Nevertheless, to be truly effective in sharing this Mina, you will need a business partner.

2. Be filled with the Spirit.

If you are to be successful in doing business with the Mina, you need a business partner! Luke gives us the very last words Jesus told his disciples before He ascended into Heaven:

"While staying with them, he ordered them not to depart from Jerusalem but to wait for the promise of the Father, which he said, 'You heard from me; for John baptized with water, but you will be baptized with the Holy Spirit not many days from now.'"[38]

Then He says:

"But you will receive power when the Holy Spirit has come upon you, and you will be my witnesses . . . ."[39]

So Jesus commands them to do business with the Mina, but then says, "DON'T YOU DARE START THIS BUSINESS UNTIL YOU RECEIVE THE POWER NECESSARY THROUGH THE BAPTISM WITH THE HOLY SPIRIT."

That seems straightforward. I find it sad that we accept the Lord's promise of Salvation without too many questions, but when He offers us another Promise, the gift of the Holy

---

38   Acts 1:4, 5

39   Acts 1:8

Spirit for power in witnessing and signs and wonders, we throw up our arms collectively and say, "No thanks!"

There are denominations, ministries, books, and YouTube channels that will argue incessantly that speaking in tongues is from the devil and signs and wonders are unnecessary. They explain away every verse that pertains to any supernatural ministry of the Spirit.

With what consequences? The servants of the Lord struggle to live in holiness, are ashamed of the cross, and are afraid to share about Jesus for fear of rejection and man's opinion. A small percentage of the professing Church say they have shared the Gospel.

It is time we get excited about Jesus's promise! The Holy Spirit's immersion in our lives is given to us so we can have the power to be His witnesses.

Then Jesus promises something else. When you preach the Gospel with the power of His Spirit, He is standing by to do what He just loves to do:

"And these signs will accompany those who believe: in my name, they will cast out demons; they will speak in new tongues; they will pick up serpents with their hands; and if they drink any deadly poison, it will not hurt them; they will lay their hands on the sick, and they will recover."[40]

---

40   Mark 16:17–18

Signs and wonders will accompany the Gospel and help propel the Good News to the far corners of the earth. Remember, it is not your job to save anybody, nor is it your job to perform miracles. That is the job of the Holy Spirit. Just open the door for Him to work.

I am fully aware that this topic has been taken to extremes, and there have been manifestations of the flesh rather than the Spirit. Yet the poor testimony of some does not invalidate the beautiful promise of Jesus. My challenge to you is to be the servant of the Lord who models with a good testimony.

You will never accomplish all God has for you on your own. You must be filled with the Spirit.

3. Pray!

The Gospel Message is loaded with power.
The Holy Spirit is loaded with power.
Prayer is loaded with power.

"Ask, and you will receive."[41] "Whatever you ask in my name, I will do."[42]

---

41   Matthew 7:7

42   John 14:13

Prayer is powerful because when you spend time with the all-powerful God, He will share strategies for your business and allow you to access His ideas and creativity.

When you pray that God's kingdom would come and His will would be done on earth as it is in Heaven, that is precisely what He wants to do! How is He not going to answer that prayer? You pray, God hears, and God answers. That is powerful.

Yet all this power is dormant if you remain on the couch.

4. Get off the couch!

You need to activate—obey, move, speak. Obedience is what differentiates you as a faithful servant from an unfaithful servant. God has given you a powerful message that can change people's hearts and eternal destinies. He has also given you many abilities to do business with the Mina. He has filled you with the Holy Spirit and placed the weapon of prayer at your disposal. Now, the only thing left for you to do is put the Mina to work and use the handkerchief to wipe the sweat of labor from your brow.[43]

---

43   C. H. Spurgeon, *Our Lord's Parables*, p. 246

The Great Commission is often translated, "Go into all the world and preach the Gospel."[44] Yet, in the original Greek, the more precise translation is, "Having gone into the world, *preach* the Gospel." "Preach" is the imperative (command) verb, not "go." You see, you are already going! **As you go** to the supermarket, **as you go** to work, **as you go** to school, **as you go** to the gas station, share the Gospel. Invest the Mina.

To multiply the Mina successfully, you will need these four areas of power: **the Gospel Message, The Holy Spirit, Prayer,** and **Obedience**.

Before we conclude this book, I have one more question.

---

44   Mark 16:15

CHAPTER 16

WHERE ARE THE OTHER SEVEN SERVANTS?

The nobleman called ten servants and gave each a Mina. Yet we have only heard how it went for three of them.

Where are the other seven servants?

Could one of the seven be holding this book in their hands right now?

This story still needs to be completed. Jesus has yet to receive the fullness of His kingdom, and some enemies still need to be warned and told of the Good News.

The results of **your Mina business** and how much profit you can secure for your Lord have yet to be determined. But it is not too late. Are Ten Minas the limit? I don't see why they should be. Could you not live your life intentionally and amp up your Mina business and be that servant who produces thirty, sixty, or a hundred-times as much?[45]

God has entrusted us with the best He has: His Gospel Message and the presence of His Holy Spirit! This treasure is in our hands and hearts. Even though He knows we are fallible, we are stewards of something that belongs to Him, so what will we do about it? When you die and are called before God to give an account of what you did with the Mina, what will you present to the Nobleman?

---

45   Matthew 13:23

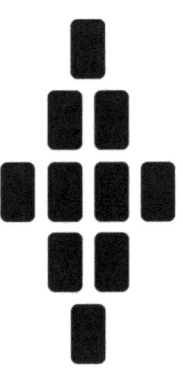

QUESTIONS TO PONDER

- What does the "Mina" represent?

- What does Jesus expect of you as a servant?

- How can you do business with the Mina?

- What happens to those who don't allow Jesus to rule their life?

- Are you a citizen or a servant?

■ Are you a faithful or an unfaithful servant?

■ What kind of servant do you want to be?

■ What talents and giftings are you using in this business?

■ How can you increase and cause your business to grow?

■ Is it more clear what God's will and mission are for your life? Write it out. "God's mission for my life is . . .

CONCLUSION

As I have decoded the mystery of this parable, I trust that you have realized your mission in life and the calling of every servant of Christ is to do business with the Mina. You don't need a "special call" to talk to people about Jesus. He calls us *all* to share the Gospel—to get His message out to everyone.

Now you know about the Mina and understand that God has given you talents to share His Gospel message. Too many still need to learn about Jesus and what He did on the cross for them. Tell them.

The Mina needs a vehicle to work, so use your hands, feet, and mouth to give them the best news ever. They do not have to die in their sins. They can be forgiven. Hand them a Mina and watch the Lord work in their lives.

Thank you for reading this book.

What is your next step?

1. We would love for you to connect to **Minabusiness.org** and join the movement of faithful servants. You can share your stories, ideas, and testimonies.

2. I have also written another book, *The Power of the Gospel*, which further explains the message of the cross.

3. If you want training on how to share the Gospel easily and creatively, we have a fantastic course that will teach you how to be more effective in your Mina business. Connect with us at **www.ontheredbox.org**. You can do the course individually or as a group. We want to equip you to be more effective in doing business with the Mina!